LEARN TO DRAW... ANIMALS!

By Mara Conlon

Illustrated by Kerren Barbas Steckler

Designed by Heather Zschock

D0166502

 PETER PAUPER PRESS, INC.
White Plains, New York

For the little Stecklers

PETER PAUPER PRESS

In 1928, at the age of twenty-two, Peter Beilenson began printing books on a small press in the basement of his parents' home in Larchmont, New York. Peter—and later, his wife, Edna—sought to create fine books that sold at "prices even a pauper could afford."

Today, still family owned and operated, Peter Pauper Press continues to honor our founders' legacy of quality, value, and fun for big kids and small kids alike.

Illustrations copyright © 2015 Kerren Barbas Steckler
Designed by Heather Zschock

Copyright © 2015
Peter Pauper Press, Inc.
Manufactured for Peter Pauper Press, Inc.
202 Mamaroneck Avenue
White Plains, NY 10601
ISBN 978-1-4413-0270-0
Printed in China

Published in the United Kingdom and Europe by
Peter Pauper Press, Inc., c/o White Pebble International
Unit 2, Plot 11 Terminus Road
Chichester, West Sussex PO19 8TX, UK

21

Hey, young artists!

Are you ready to learn how to draw 45 different animals? It's easy and fun! Just follow these steps:

First, pick an animal you want to draw. (You might want to start with the snake . . . he's pretty ssssimple.)

Next, trace over the animal with a pencil. This will give you a feel for how to draw the lines.

Then, following the numbered boxes, start drawing each new step (shown in red) of the animal in the empty space in each scene, or on a piece of paper.

Lastly, if you're an awesome artist (and of course, you are!), try drawing a whole scene with one or more of the animals. And remember, don't worry if your drawings look different from the ones in this book—no two animals are exactly alike!

You're on your way to creating wild, furry, and fuzzy masterpieces!

GET READY! GET SET! DRAW!

Snake

1.

2.

3.

4.

Prairie dog

1.

2.

3.

4.

5.

6.

Puppy

1.
2.
3.
4.
5.
6.

Poodle

1.
2.
3.
4.
5.
6.

DOG PARK

Trace over me for practice!

Bunny

1.

2.

3.

4.

5.

6.

Chick

1.

2.

3.

4.

5.

6.

Bear

1.

2.

3.

4.

5.

6.

Fox

1.

2.

3.

4.

5.

6.

Trace over me
for practice!

Songbird

1.

2.

3.

4.

5.

6.

Parrot

1.

2.

3.

4.

5.

6.

Trace over me for practice!

Butterfly

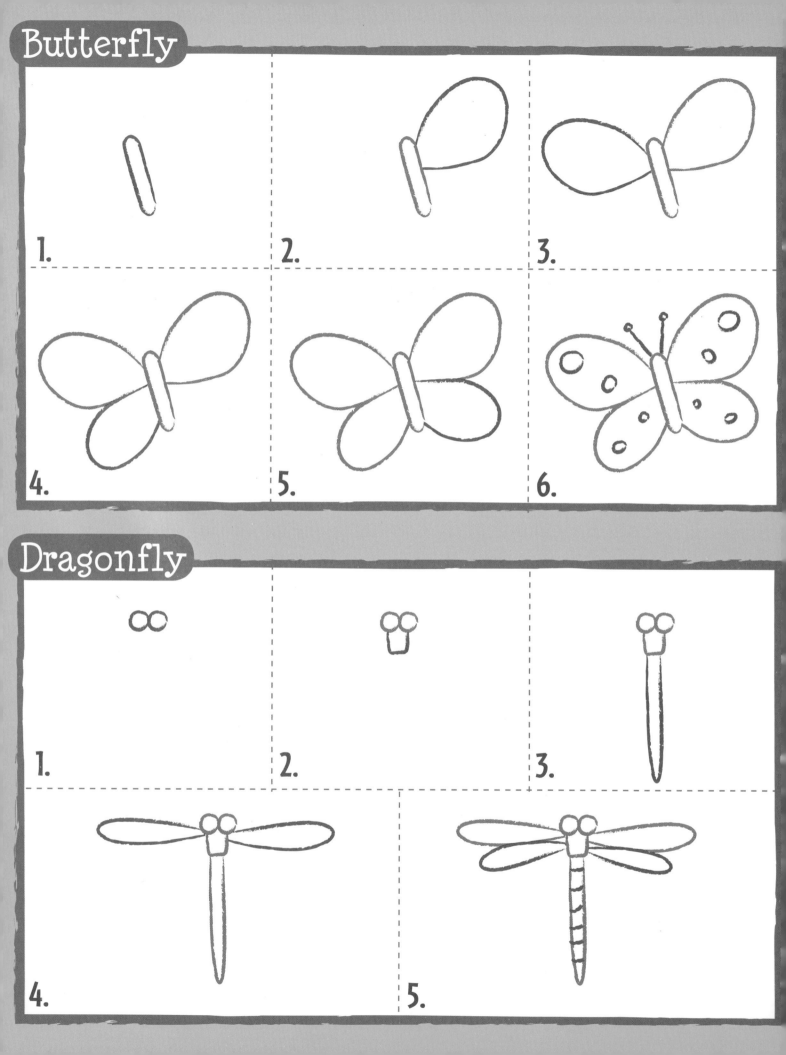

1.
2.
3.
4.
5.
6.

Dragonfly

1.
2.
3.
4.
5.

Trace over me for practice!

Horse

1.

2.

3.

4.

5.

6.

Sheep

1.

2.

3.

4.

5.

6.

Pig

1.

2.

3.

4.

5.

6.

Cow

1.

2.

3.

4.

5.

6.

Camel

1.

2.

3.

4.

5.

Armadillo

1.

2.

3.

4.

Elephant

1.
2.
3.
4.
5.
6.

Lion

1.
2.
3.
4.
5.
6.

Draw more like me below!

Giraffe

1.

2.

3.

4.

Zebra

1.

2.

3.

4.

5.

6.

Penguin

1.

2.

3.

4.

5.

6.

Polar bear

1.

2.

3.

4.

5.

6.

Raccoon

1.

2.

3.

4.

5.

6.

Owl

1.

2.

3.

4.

5.

6.

Fish

1.
2.
3.
4.
5.
6.

Seahorse

1.
2.
3.
4.
5.
6.

Hippo

1.

2.

3.

4.

5.

6.

Crocodile

1.

2.

3.

4.

Cat

1.

2.

3.

4.

5.

6.

Mouse

1.

2.

3.

4.

Monkey

1.
2.
3.
4.
5.
6.

Gorilla

1.
2.
3.
4.
5.
6.

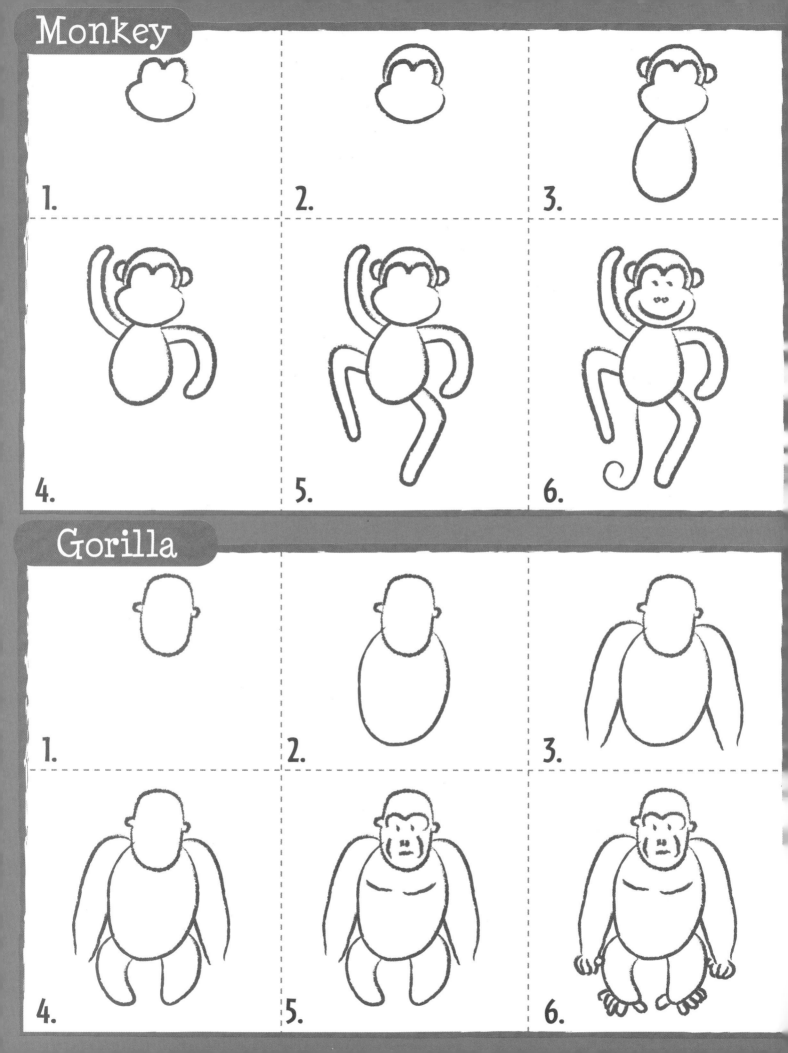

Whale

1.

2.

3.

4.

5.

6.

Seal

1.

2.

3.

4.

5.

6.

Turtle

1.

2.

3.

4.

5.

6.

Bee

1.

2.

3.

4.

5.

6.

Ladybug

1.

2.

3.

4.

5.

6.

Trace over me for practice!

Koala

1.

2.

3.

4.

5.

6.

Kangaroo

1.

2.

3.

4.

5.

6.

Rhinoceros

1.

2.

3.

4.

5.

6.

Flamingo

1.

2.

3.

4.

5.

6.

Squirrel

1.

2.

3.

4.

5.

6.

Hedgehog

1.

2.

3.

4.

5.

6.

We drew a whole zoo.
And now, you can too!